STECK-VAUGHN

COMPREHENSION SKILLS

FACTS

LEVEL F

Linda Ward Beech

Tara McCarthy

Donna Townsend

STECK-VAUGHN
ELEMENTARY · SECONDARY · ADULT · LIBRARY

A Harcourt Company

www.steck-vaughn.com

Editorial Director:	Diane Schnell
Project Editor:	Anne Souby
Associate Director of Design:	Cynthia Ellis
Design Manager:	Cynthia Hannon
Media Researcher:	Christina Berry
Production:	Rusty Kay
Cover Illustration:	Stephanie Carter
Cover Production:	Alan Klemp
Photograph:	©CORBIS

ISBN 0-7398-2653-0

1 2 3 4 5 6 7 8 9 0 BNG 04 03 02 01 00

Facts are things like names, dates, and places. In this book you will practice finding facts.

Sometimes you may notice more facts when you visit someplace far away from home. Then you may see unusual facts all around you. What facts can you see in the picture of the forest on this page?

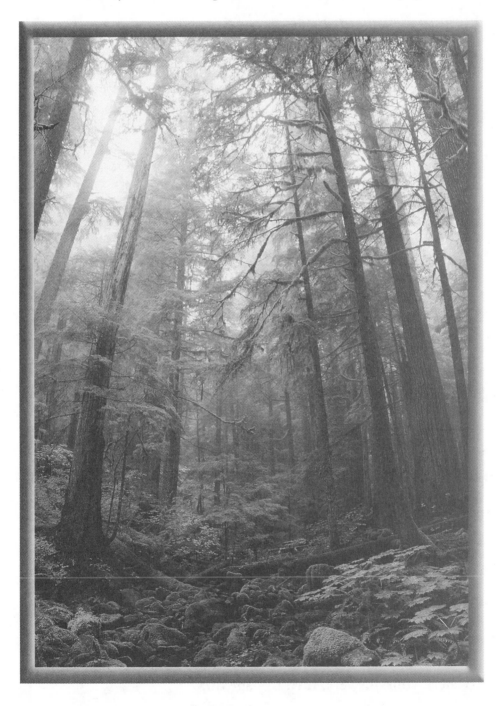

What Are Facts?

Facts are sometimes called details. They are small pieces of information. Facts can appear in true stories, such as those in the newspaper. They can also appear in legends and other stories that people make up.

How to Read for Facts

You can find facts by asking yourself questions. Ask *who*, and your answer will be a fact about a person. Ask *what*, and your answer will be a fact about a thing. Ask *where*, and your answer will be a fact about a place. Ask *when*, and your answer will be a fact about a time. Ask *how many* or *how much*, and your answer will be a fact about a number or an amount.

Try It!

Read this story and look for facts as you read. Ask yourself *when* and *who*.

◆

The First Airplane Flight

Wilbur and Orville Wright read everything they could find about flying machines. They began building their own airplane in 1899. They carefully tested every part of the airplane. Finally on a cold, windy day in December 1903, they flew their plane for the first time. Orville was the pilot as the plane lifted into the air. It stayed in the air for only 12 seconds and traveled just 120 feet the first time. After three more tries that same day, the plane's longest trip was almost a full minute and more than 850 feet.

Did you find these facts when you read the paragraph? Write the facts on the lines below.

◆ When did the Wrights fly for the first time?

Fact: _____

◆ Who was the pilot?

Fact: _____

To check your answers, turn to page 60.

Practice Finding Facts

Below are some practice questions. The first two are already answered. Answer the third one on your own.

___C___ **1.** How long was the plane's longest trip?
        A. 120 feet   **C.** 850 feet
        B. 85 feet   **D.** 12 feet

Look at the question and answers again. *How long* is asking for a number. There are many numbers in the paragraph, but you are looking for one that describes the plane's longest trip. Read the paragraph until you find the words *longest trip*. You should find this sentence: "After three more tries that same day, the plane's longest trip was almost a full minute and more than 850 feet." So **C** is the correct answer. Answer **A** is also a fact from the story, but it describes the first trip, not the longest one.

___D___ **2.** The Wright brothers first flew their plane in
        A. summer   **C.** fall
        B. spring   **D.** winter

Look at the question. The first answer you might think of is a place. But the possible answers are seasons. Search the story for words about seasons or time of year. You should find this sentence: "Finally on a cold, windy day in December 1903, they flew their plane for the first time." The correct answer is *winter*. The answer uses different words, but the fact is the same.

Now it's your turn to practice. Answer the next question by writing the letter of the correct answer on the line.

_____ **3.** The Wrights first started working on their airplane in
        A. 1903   **C.** 1908
        B. 1899   **D.** 1809

To check your answer, turn to page 60.

Using What You Know

Read the following question words and facts that answer the questions. Ask yourself the questions. Then write facts about yourself on the lines.

Who?

Mary Lou Retton won five medals at the Olympics.

Abraham Lincoln was President during the Civil War.

◆ My name is _____.

What?

The game ended in a tie.

The crowd ran onto the field.

◆ My favorite song is _____.

Where?

The bus stops on Main Street.

The Amazon River flows through Brazil.

◆ I live in the city of _____.

When?

School used to begin after Labor Day.

Columbus landed in the New World in 1492.

◆ I was born on _____.

How Many? / How Much?

The team lost 14 of their 16 games.

A panda eats 45 pounds of bamboo a day.

◆ There are _____ students in my class.

Steck-Vaughn • Comprehension Skills Series

How to Use This Book

In this book you will read 25 stories. Each story has two parts. Read the first part, then answer five questions about it. Then read the second part and answer the next five questions.

When you finish reading each story and answering the questions about it, check your answers by looking at pages 61 and 62. Write the number of correct answers in the score box at the top of the page.

Remember

This book asks questions about facts in stories. When you answer the questions, use the facts in the story. You may already know some facts about the subject, but the story will have the answers you need for the questions.

Hints for Better Reading

- Look for facts while you are reading the stories. Notice the names of people, animals, and things. Look for places, dates, and times.
- Read each question carefully. Think about the facts you need to answer the question. Try to find a sentence in the story that has some of the same words as the question.
- Try to remember the facts you read in the story. If you can't remember, look back at the story.

Challenge Yourself

Try this special challenge. Read each story. Cover the story with a sheet of paper, and try to remember the facts. Answer the questions without looking back at the story.

Writing

On pages 30 and 58, there are stories with questions. These do not have answers for you to choose. Think of an answer and write it in your own words. On pages 31 and 59, you are asked to write your own story. You are given a prewriting activity to help you. You will find suggested answers on page 60, but your answers may be very different.

Scarecrows Then and Now

Birds have always been a problem for farmers. They like to eat the seeds in farmers' fields. As soon as a farmer plants seeds, the birds arrive for dinner. Often these birds are crows.

Farmers try to get rid of their unwanted visitors by making scarecrows. A scarecrow is supposed to scare away crows and other birds. The first scarecrows were made hundreds of years ago. They were sticks stuck in the ground with big rags tied to the top. When the wind blew, the rags flapped and frightened the birds.

As time went on, farmers began making better scarecrows. They nailed a second stick across the top of the one in the ground. Now the scarecrows had arms and could wear old shirts. When farmers stuffed the shirts with straw, the scarecrows began to look like real people. Some even had faces.

_____ **1.** Birds like to eat
   A. fields   **C.** rags
   B. seeds   **D.** sticks

_____ **2.** A scarecrow is supposed to scare away
   A. gardens   **C.** birds
   B. seeds   **D.** sticks

_____ **3.** The first scarecrows were made from sticks and
   A. rags   **C.** rugs
   B. plants   **D.** hats

_____ **4.** Later, farmers filled scarecrows with
   A. cotton   **C.** straw
   B. air   **D.** string

_____ **5.** Scarecrows flapped because of the
   A. arms   **C.** birds
   B. noise   **D.** wind

When farmers began using modern machines, they didn't need scarecrows anymore. The new farm machines were big and made a lot of noise. They scared the birds away quite well.

In the 1960s people became interested in folk art such as scarecrows. Suddenly scarecrows were popular again. People wanted them for their yards and vegetable gardens. Even people in cities bought scarecrows for their porches.

Today some artists make scarecrows to sell. They use natural materials such as sticks and straw for the bodies. However, these new scarecrows are often dressed in fancy clothes. Some wear sunglasses, belts, or scarves. Some scarecrows may have beads, flowers, and purses.

_____ **6.** People didn't need scarecrows because they had
    A. clothes   **C.** workers
    B. machines   **D.** crows

_____ **7.** In the 1960s people thought that scarecrows were
    A. folk art   **C.** farm workers
    B. sunglasses   **D.** fine art

_____ **8.** People put scarecrows on porches and in
    A. machines   **C.** yards
    B. cities   **D.** parks

_____ **9.** Today some artists make scarecrows for
    A. sale   **C.** sail
    B. beads   **D.** style

_____ **10.** Scarecrows sometimes have beads, flowers, and
    A. ties   **C.** pins
    B. shoes   **D.** purses

Basketball Begins

Basketball is the only major sport that is a totally American game. Jim Naismith started it all. During the 1880s Naismith taught athletics at a college in Massachusetts.

In the fall Naismith's students spent long, exciting hours on the football field. But when winter came, the students moved indoors and did exercises. Most students soon grew bored. They kept asking for an indoor game that was as exciting as football.

Naismith began to think about a new kind of ball game that could be played safely in a small gym. He decided that players wouldn't use bats or run while holding the ball. Players would use only their hands to pass or throw the ball to other players. Naismith still had one big question. How would players score points? He went to the college storeroom and pulled out two peach baskets!

_____ **1.** Jim Naismith was a teacher of
  A. history   **C.** athletics
  B. science   **D.** safety

_____ **2.** The students wanted an indoor
  A. game   **C.** exercise
  B. gym   **D.** coach

_____ **3.** In the new game, players would not use
  A. hands   **C.** bats
  B. goals   **D.** teams

_____ **4.** Players would pass or
  A. hit the ball   **C.** punch the ball
  B. throw the ball   **D.** kick the ball

_____ **5.** Naismith had a question about how players would
  A. find peach baskets   **C.** stay safe
  B. run with the ball   **D.** score points

There was a balcony all around the gym. It was exactly ten feet above the floor. Naismith hung one peach basket on the balcony at each end of the gym. Then he divided the class into two teams of nine players each. The first basketball game began when he threw a soccer ball up between the team captains.

The players dashed up and down the gym. They yelled with excitement as they tried to throw the ball into the peach baskets. The game stopped for a while when one player finally sank the ball. Someone climbed a ladder to get it out. After all, there is no hole in the bottom of a peach basket! But that was the only pause in this first basketball game. The final score was 1–0.

As basketball became popular at other colleges, teams made up their own rules. However, a set of rules was developed within a few years. A special ball and an open hoop took the place of the soccer ball and peach baskets. The game of basketball had begun.

_____ **6.** The baskets were at a height of ten feet because of the
    A. floor   **C.** peaches
    B. balcony   **D.** ball

_____ **7.** Naismith's basketball teams were composed of
    A. nine players   **C.** fifty players
    B. thirty players   **D.** five players

_____ **8.** For a while the game was played with a
    A. basketball   **C.** football
    B. soccer ball   **D.** baseball

_____ **9.** The first baskets were
    A. filled with peaches   **C.** open at the bottom
    B. made from ladders   **D.** closed at the bottom

_____ **10.** For the first few years, basketball teams used
    A. Naismith's rules   **C.** their own rules
    B. today's rules   **D.** no rules

UNIT 3

The Altamira Paintings

As early as 20,000 years ago, people painted pictures on the walls of caves. Many of the paintings were later found by people exploring the caves. Some are in places that can be reached only on hands and knees.

In 1879 a man and his daughter went into one of these caves in northern Spain. The man held a lighted candle as they made their way deep into the darkness. Suddenly his daughter shouted, "Toros! Toros!" ("Bulls! Bulls!") He looked up to see paintings of bison, or buffalo, on the cave's walls. The girl had found what are now known as the Altamira paintings. They are the most famous cave paintings in the world.

_____ **1.** People painted on the walls of caves as early as
  A. 30,000 years ago **C.** 2,000 years ago
  B. 20,000 years ago **D.** 10,000 years ago

_____ **2.** Some paintings can be reached only by using
  A. a car **C.** a train or bus
  B. a rope **D.** hands and knees

_____ **3.** The Altamira paintings were found in
  A. 1879 **C.** 89
  B. 1789 **D.** 789

_____ **4.** To find his way, the man used
  A. a flashlight **C.** a candle
  B. a string **D.** radar

_____ **5.** The girl saw paintings of
  A. bison **C.** caves
  B. horses **D.** people

Steck-Vaughn • Comprehension Skills Series

The people who had painted these remarkable pictures had worked deep inside the cave where there is no light. Yet they had painted many exact details of the animals' bodies. Experts think that they burned fat in stone lamps to light their work. They also think that the painters may have dragged the animals they painted into the caves.

No one knows why the artists went to so much trouble. But many people think that the paintings were part of a ceremony to bring good luck before a big hunt. The paintings show many wounded or dying animals. Others are shown swimming in a river where they would have been easy to catch.

_____ **6.** The caves where the artists worked were
    A. peaceful   **C.** dark
    B. windy   **D.** comfortable

_____ **7.** Many details in the paintings are
    A. sketchy   **C.** very faded
    B. exact   **D.** too large

_____ **8.** To help them paint details, the artists may have used
    A. sketches   **C.** small brushes
    B. strong colors   **D.** animals as models

_____ **9.** Perhaps the artists felt that painting helped them to
    A. farm   **C.** hunt
    B. sleep   **D.** swim

_____ **10.** In the paintings the animals appear
    A. weak   **C.** wild
    B. strong   **D.** hungry

What's Cooking?

People can learn history from cookbooks. Old cookbooks tell what foods people ate long ago. The books may also tell about eating customs.

One large collection of cookbooks is in Washington, D.C. It is part of the Library of Congress. This library belongs to the people of the United States. There are more than 6,500 cookbooks in its collection. Most of them are very old and rare. Some are one of a kind.

The oldest cookbook at this library was written in 1475. It was written in Latin. It has 12 recipes for cooking fish. It also tells how to make many vegetable dishes. The famous Italian artist Leonardo da Vinci might have used this book. He did not eat meat.

_____ **1.** One thing people can learn from a cookbook is
- **A.** vegetables
- **B.** reading
- **C.** history
- **D.** science

_____ **2.** Cookbooks are records of people's foods and
- **A.** customs
- **B.** clothes
- **C.** materials
- **D.** collections

_____ **3.** The Library of Congress is in
- **A.** Italy
- **B.** Latin
- **C.** Europe
- **D.** Washington, D.C.

_____ **4.** The oldest cookbook in the library was written in
- **A.** 1475
- **B.** 1745
- **C.** 1986
- **D.** 1400

_____ **5.** This cookbook has 12 recipes for
- **A.** meat
- **B.** soup
- **C.** stew
- **D.** fish

Steck-Vaughn • Comprehension Skills Series

The cookbooks at the Library of Congress trace cooking for five hundred years. The oldest cookbooks show that food wasn't as important to people as it is now. Long ago, eating was just something that people did in order to live. Later, people began to think of food as something to enjoy. Recipes became fancier. Food took more time to prepare.

Cookbooks from the 1700s show that people began to care more about how they served meals. These cookbooks have pages on how to fold napkins. They also show how to carve a goose or peel an orange.

Who uses these old cookbooks today? Suppose you were writing a story about the 1600s. You might want information on what people ate then. Or suppose you were a scientist studying a certain fruit. You might want to know when that fruit was first used. Old cookbooks are a record of the past.

_____ **6.** Long ago, people just ate to stay
      A. full   **C.** sick
      B. alive   **D.** home

_____ **7.** In time, people thought of food as
      A. something to do   **C.** something to learn
      B. something to enjoy **D.** something to happen

_____ **8.** As recipes became fancier, food took longer to
      A. eat   **C.** prepare
      B. write   **D.** serve

_____ **9.** In the 1700s cookbooks told how to
      A. wash napkins   **C.** fold chairs
      B. fold napkins   **D.** set tables

_____ **10.** Writers and scientists of today use old cookbooks for
      A. review   **C.** cooking
      B. imagination   **D.** information

UNIT 5

The Underground City

Toronto has the world's largest shopping mall under the ground. It has more than one thousand shops and services. They are joined by miles of tunnels and sidewalks.

These tunnels and sidewalks also join more than thirty high-rise buildings. To get to the underground mall, shoppers go in one of the buildings and ride the elevator down. People can also take the subway to other parts of the city.

The city-under-the-city is always a pleasant place to walk. That's because the temperature is controlled. Outside, winter may be cold or summer may be hot. But deep down in the mall, the temperature stays the same all year round.

_____ 1. The largest underground mall is in
    A. City Hall   **C.** Toronto
    B. New York   **D.** an office building

_____ 2. In the shopping mall, there are more than one thousand
    A. tunnels and sidewalks   **C.** business workers
    B. shops and services   **D.** underground trains

_____ 3. The tunnels and sidewalks connect
    A. thousands of tourists   **C.** cities in Canada
    B. all parts of Toronto   **D.** more than thirty buildings

_____ 4. To get to other parts of Toronto, people take
    A. tunnels   **C.** subways
    B. sidewalks   **D.** elevators

_____ 5. The mall temperature is always
    A. different   **C.** outside
    B. the same   **D.** interesting

A city underground might be dark and gloomy. But Toronto's underground city is not that way at all. There are many bright lights. Shops are trimmed with polished metal and gleaming glass. Parts of the mall are on three levels. The levels are joined by stairs and elevators. Flowers and trees grow along the sidewalks.

The underground mall has more than shops. It has paintings and other works of art. It has theaters that give plays and concerts.

The city-under-the-city was so popular that Toronto business people began to worry! They wanted visitors to see Toronto at street level, too. So an aboveground mall was built at Eaton Centre. It has about three hundred stores, several movie houses, and many restaurants.

_____ **6.** The underground mall is
    A. gloomy   **C.** empty
    B. dark   **D.** bright

_____ **7.** In the underground mall, you can shop and
    A. go to concerts   **C.** take art classes
    B. see Eaton Centre   **D.** buy glass

_____ **8.** To get to different levels of the mall, you can use
    A. subways   **C.** sidewalks
    B. stairways   **D.** areas

_____ **9.** The Eaton Centre mall is
    A. under the ground   **C.** above the buildings
    B. at street level   **D.** outside the city

_____**10.** Eaton Centre was built because
    A. a mall was needed   **C.** businesses wanted it
    B. stores were needed   **D.** Toronto was popular

Merry-Go-Rounds

The organ starts, and its music fills the air. The horses slowly begin to move. Riders hold tightly as their colorful horses go up and down and around and around. These riders are on a carousel. *Carousel* is another word for *merry-go-round*.

Carousels have a long history. In the 1400s soldiers in France liked to play a ball game on horseback. The soldiers had to throw and catch while their horses were moving. The French invented a way to help the soldiers practice for the game.

This invention was the first carousel. It was different from modern carousels. The biggest difference was that the horses were real! They turned the carousel as they moved in a circle. Years later, people began using carousels for fun. By the 1800s carousel horses were no longer real. Carousels were run by motors.

_____ **1.** *Merry-go-round* is another word for
    A. ferris wheel   **C.** roller coaster
    B. moving horse   **D.** carousel

_____ **2.** The music for carousels comes from
    A. riders   **C.** pianos
    B. organs   **D.** radios

_____ **3.** The first carousel was made to help players
    A. fight wars   **C.** ride horses
    B. invent tricks   **D.** practice skills

_____ **4.** The horses on the first carousels were
    A. real   **C.** painted
    B. wood   **D.** motors

_____ **5.** The first people to use a carousel were
    A. inventors   **C.** soldiers
    B. sailors   **D.** children

Once there were ten thousand merry-go-rounds in the United States. Most were made in Pennsylvania and New York. Workers carved and painted the carousel horses. Some horses had fine saddles and roses around their necks. Others had a wild look in their shiny glass eyes. No two horses were the same.

Today there are fewer than three hundred merry-go-rounds in North America. Some of these rides are now treasured as historic places.

One of the nation's oldest merry-go-rounds is in Oak Bluffs, Massachusetts. This carousel is called the Flying Horses. It was built around 1880. Riders on the Flying Horses can have some extra fun. As the merry-go-round spins, they try to grab rings from a post on the wall. The person who gets the most rings is the winner. The reward is a free ride.

_____ **6.** No two carousel horses were
       A. bright   **C.** carved
       B. wild   **D.** alike

_____ **7.** One state where carousels were made was
       A. Massachusetts   **C.** France
       B. Pennsylvania   **D.** Oak Bluffs

_____ **8.** Some carousels are now considered to be
       A. too fast   **C.** historic
       B. dangerous   **D.** too small

_____ **9.** One of America's oldest carousels is called the
       A. Oak Bluffs   **C.** Fighting Horses
       B. Flying Horses   **D.** New York

_____ **10.** A free ride on this merry-go-round is given as a
       A. prize   **C.** ring
       B. horse   **D.** win

Happy Birthday!

Giant sequoia trees grow near the coast of northern California. Sequoia trees are also called redwoods. For many years experts thought that these tall trees were the oldest living trees on Earth. In 1892 one of the trees was cut down. Scientists counted the growth rings in the tree to find out its age. They discovered that the tree was indeed old. It had lived for about 3,212 years. Today experts know that the redwood trees average about 3,500 years in age.

Redwood trees have straight trunks and branches that seem to brush against the sky. One redwood, named "General Sherman," is the tallest living thing in the world. It is more than 275 feet tall.

_____ 1. Redwood trees are also called
   A. oak trees   C. cedars
   B. elm trees   D. sequoias

_____ 2. Experts once thought the redwoods were the
   A. youngest trees   C. tallest trees
   B. oldest trees   D. prettiest trees

_____ 3. To find out the age of a tree, scientists count its
   A. rings   C. trunks
   B. leaves   D. branches

_____ 4. In 1892 a redwood was discovered to be
   A. 212 years old   C. 3,212 years old
   B. 215 years old   D. 2,012 years old

_____ 5. "General Sherman" is more than
   A. 275 feet tall   C. 727 feet tall
   B. 288 feet tall   D. 342 feet tall

In 1953 scientists became interested in another type of tree. They had discovered some very old bristlecone pines in Nevada. At heights of only 20 to 60 feet, these pines were not as grand as the redwoods. But the experts began to wonder if they were older.

In 1957 they found a bristlecone pine that was more than 4,000 years old. Their theory had been correct. Further study turned up even older trees. One of these trees, "Methuselah," is the oldest living tree in the world. It is about 4,700 years old. But even though the pines are older, they may not live as long as the redwoods. This is because the redwoods have a longer life span.

_____ **6.** In 1953 scientists became interested in another
        A. state   **C.** pine cone
        B. wildflower   **D.** type of tree

_____ **7.** Experts discovered some pine trees that were
        A. dying   **C.** very old
        B. tall   **D.** useful

_____ **8.** Compared to redwoods, pine trees are not as
        A. tall   **C.** healthy
        B. rough   **D.** green

_____ **9.** The oldest living tree in the world is
        A. a redwood   **C.** Methuselah
        B. a sequoia   **D.** General Sherman

_____ **10.** Although the pines are older, the redwoods will
        A. die soon   **C.** live longer
        B. live forever   **D.** stay small

How to Win a Prize

There are all kinds of contests. Have you ever heard of the Apple Seed Popping Contest? It's held on the first weekend in October in Lincoln, Nebraska. How does it work? Line up with everybody else. Take a fresh apple, and squeeze it hard in your fist. If your apple seeds pop the farthest, you're a winner!

Do you like food contests? Every August in Fulton, Kentucky, there's a banana contest. If you eat the most bananas within a set time, you win some more bananas. If you like milk, go to Los Angeles, California, in September. Sign up for the Milk Drinking Contest. If you win, you get a ribbon.

In Albany, Oregon, anyone between the ages of 5 and 12 can enter the Bubble Gum Blowing Contest. You'll win some books if you blow the first bubble, the biggest bubble, or the bubble that lasts the longest.

_____ **1.** The Apple Seed Popping Contest is held in
- **A.** California
- **B.** October
- **C.** August
- **D.** Albany

_____ **2.** To win the Apple Seed Popping Contest, you must
- **A.** be under 16
- **B.** line up the seeds
- **C.** pop seeds the farthest
- **D.** squeeze the fresh apple

_____ **3.** The winner of the banana contest gets
- **A.** a set time
- **B.** a ribbon
- **C.** more bananas
- **D.** a trip to Fulton

_____ **4.** People who like milk could sign up for a contest in
- **A.** Los Angeles
- **B.** Nebraska
- **C.** Oregon
- **D.** Kentucky

_____ **5.** The person who blows the biggest bubble wins
- **A.** gum
- **B.** food
- **C.** books
- **D.** bikes

Some contests require a special animal. In May bring your chicken to the Chicken Flying Meet in Rio Grande, Ohio. Put your chicken on the launch pad. At the signal, give it a little push. If your chicken flies the farthest, you win a cash prize.

People 14 and under can enter the Greasy Pig Scramble in Dothan, Alabama. The pigs are greased with peanut oil. You have to catch the greasy pig and hold on to it until it crosses the finish line. If you win, you get the pig.

If you have a pet crab, you can enter it in the World Championship Crab Race in California. The International Frog Jumping and Racing Contest is held in Louisiana. Winners of both contests get medals. Petaluma, California, holds an Ugly Dog Contest. The winners receive medals and are invited to come back next year for the Ugliest Dog Contest.

_____ **6.** In some contests, you need a pet that is
    A. slow   **C.** afraid
    B. prized   **D.** unusual

_____ **7.** The Chicken Flying Meet is in
    A. Ohio   **C.** California
    B. Alabama   **D.** Louisiana

_____ **8.** In the Dothan, Alabama, contest you have to
    A. use peanuts   **C.** count pigs
    B. hold on   **D.** push chickens

_____ **9.** Louisiana has a special contest for
    A. frogs   **C.** crabs
    B. dogs   **D.** pigs

_____ **10.** The Ugliest Dog Contest is for dogs that
    A. are not strange   **C.** won the year before
    B. live in Ohio   **D.** like to get medals

Ray Wins the Gold!
Ten Times!

When he was a child, Ray Ewry became ill with a fever. His doctors told him that he had polio. Polio is a disease that causes people to become paralyzed. Ray gradually got better, but he found that his legs had been weakened by his illness. The doctors thought that leg exercises might help him regain his strength. But they told Ray that he probably would never be able to walk and run as he once had.

For the next few years, Ray exercised daily. He did everything his doctors had recommended and more. After a while he could tell that his hard work was paying off. His legs became stronger and stronger. He even began to take part in track and field events.

_____ **1.** The disease that Ray Ewry had was
     A. the measles   **C.** polio
     B. chicken pox   **D.** tuberculosis

_____ **2.** When he got better, Ray found that his legs were
     A. stronger   **C.** longer
     B. weaker   **D.** broken

_____ **3.** Doctors told Ray that he would not be able to
     A. sleep   **C.** walk and run
     B. eat   **D.** lift heavy things

_____ **4.** For the next few years, Ray exercised
     A. every two weeks   **C.** weekly
     B. once a month   **D.** daily

_____ **5.** Ray began to take part in
     A. track and field   **C.** football
     B. swimming   **D.** soccer

Soon Ray could jump higher and farther than most people. So he signed up for three contests in the 1900 Olympics. He entered the standing high jump, the standing long jump, and the standing hop, step, and jump. He won gold medals, or first place, in all three events.

Ray repeated his amazing feat in 1904 and planned to try again in 1906. But before the next games, the hop, step, and jump was dropped from the list of events. So Ray had to settle for only two gold medals in 1906 and two again in 1908. Ray had indeed overcome his illness. Today he holds the record for the most gold medals ever given to any one person.

_____ **6.** Soon Ray became very
    A. shy   **C.** skilled
    B. tired   **D.** bored

_____ **7.** In the 1900 Olympics, Ray entered
    A. jumping contests   **C.** pole vaulting
    B. running contests   **D.** five contests

_____ **8.** In 1900 Ray won gold medals in
    A. one event   **C.** three events
    B. two events   **D.** four events

_____ **9.** In the 1906 games, the hop, step, and jump was
    A. held twice   **C.** won
    B. dropped   **D.** thrilling

_____ **10.** Ray holds the record for the most
    A. jumps   **C.** gold medals
    B. events   **D.** Olympics

A Symbol of Freedom

Harriet Tubman was born a slave in Maryland around 1820. As a child she learned all about the woods from her father. As a teen she tried to stop her master from beating another slave. The master gave Harriet a bad head wound. This treatment made her want to run away to freedom.

In 1844 Tubman married a man named John who was a freed slave. Five years later she used her knowledge of the woods to escape her master's home. She fled to Philadelphia by way of the Underground Railroad. The Underground Railroad was a network of people who secretly helped runaway slaves. The runaways slept and ate in the people's homes during the day. Then they continued along their path to freedom each night.

_____ **1.** Harriet Tubman was born around
- **A.** 1844
- **B.** 1920
- **C.** 1820
- **D.** 1830

_____ **2.** She was taught about the woods by her
- **A.** master
- **B.** brothers
- **C.** mother
- **D.** father

_____ **3.** Tubman's master gave her
- **A.** a bad head wound
- **B.** her freedom
- **C.** a new master
- **D.** a new job

_____ **4.** The Underground Railroad was a network of people who helped
- **A.** new masters
- **B.** sick patients
- **C.** runaway slaves
- **D.** lost travelers

_____ **5.** Tubman fled to
- **A.** Maryland
- **B.** the South
- **C.** Philadelphia
- **D.** her slave home

Tubman did not want just her own freedom, though. She wished to help other slaves gain freedom as well. The next year she returned to Maryland to lead other slaves to Philadelphia. Her mission was very risky because a new law made it a crime to help runaway slaves. But Tubman knew that what she was doing was right. She made 18 more trips in the next ten years. She helped more than 300 slaves escape.

Over the years word of Tubman's deeds spread. She became the best-known leader of the Underground Railroad. Later Tubman also aided in the Civil War. She was a nurse, scout, and spy for the Union Army. After the war she raised money for African American schools. Today she is still a symbol of freedom around the world.

_____ **6.** Tubman returned to Maryland in order to
    A. get her clothes   **C.** get her husband
    B. free more slaves   **D.** visit her family

_____ **7.** A new law made it a crime to
    A. help masters   **C.** help slaves escape
    B. attack slaves   **D.** work as a slave

_____ **8.** In 18 trips Tubman freed more than
    A. 200 slaves   **C.** 50 slaves
    B. 100 slaves   **D.** 300 slaves

_____ **9.** Tubman helped in
    A. World War I   **C.** the Revolutionary War
    B. World War II   **D.** the Civil War

_____ **10.** Tubman served as a nurse, scout, and
    A. teacher   **C.** spy
    B. soldier   **D.** sailor

The Famous Pie Plate

In the 1880s William Frisbie and his sister were working hard at their pie business in Connecticut. She baked the pies. He took them to customers. The pies came in special metal plates called pie tins. Each tin had the words *Frisbie's Pies* on the bottom. The students at Yale University liked Frisbie pies. They liked Frisbie pie tins even better. They made up a game called Pie Tin Catch. With a flick of the wrist, they could send a pie tin flying. But people could get hurt if they were hit with a tin. So students yelled the warning "Frisbie!" as they tossed it.

In 1948 a man named William Morrison saw that Americans were fascinated by pictures and stories about strange space ships. They were called flying saucers. So Morrison designed a plastic toy in that shape. He called it a Pluto Platter. Soon Pluto Platters were flying all over beaches and parks.

_____ **1.** The Frisbies delivered
    A. bridges   **C.** businesses
    B. toys   **D.** pies

_____ **2.** The students at Yale liked
    A. studying   **C.** customers
    B. tests   **D.** pies

_____ **3.** Pie Tin Catch was a
    A. label   **C.** warning
    B. game   **D.** saucer

_____ **4.** In 1948 Americans were interested in
    A. toys   **C.** pies
    B. flying saucers   **D.** parks

_____ **5.** Morrison's toys were made of
    A. plastic   **C.** shapes
    B. Pluto   **D.** photos

In 1955 Richard Knerr and Spud Mulligan started a toy company. They bought the rights to the Pluto Platter. But for a while, the Pluto Platter lost its popularity to another toy called the Hula Hoop. People all over America were spinning hoops instead of throwing Pluto Platters.

Knerr found out about the old game called Frisbieing. He decided to give the Pluto Platter its original name. But he spelled it *Frisbee* by mistake. In the early 1960s, people got tired of Hula Hoops. They wanted to play with flying plastic saucers again. Today there are Frisbees that glow in the dark and cloth Frisbees that can be tucked in a pocket. Foam-rubber Frisbees are used indoors. The Frisbie pies may be forgotten, but Frisbees are here to stay.

_____ **6.** Knerr and Mulligan started a
- **A.** new game
- **B.** plate business
- **C.** toy company
- **D.** pie business

_____ **7.** The Hula Hoop was a special kind of
- **A.** dance
- **B.** exercise
- **C.** toy
- **D.** tin

_____ **8.** Knerr learned about
- **A.** college students
- **B.** selling Frisbees
- **C.** family names
- **D.** an old game

_____ **9.** In the 1960s people wanted
- **A.** to be indoors
- **B.** flying toys
- **C.** bigger hoops
- **D.** cloth Frisbees

_____ **10.** Foam-rubber Frisbees can be used in
- **A.** the house
- **B.** a pocket
- **C.** the dark
- **D.** plastic

The Birth of an Island

It was a gray November day in 1963. A fishing boat rocked in the Atlantic Ocean off the southern coast of Iceland. Suddenly a great black cloud burst from the water. Loud noises rumbled from the ocean, too. The ship's captain sent out a radio call. Something very unusual was happening!

In the next three hours, scientists and reporters arrived at the scene. By now the cloud was 12,000 feet high. Huge explosions sent ash, dust, and hot rocks into the air. The watchers could see something just under the water's surface.

By that night a new mountain had pushed itself up from the boiling sea. The mountain continued to rise during the next days. It also grew wider. A fiery island was growing in the Atlantic. It was caused by a volcano in the ocean.

_____ **1.** The fishing boat was off the coast of
    A. Ireland   **C.** Iceland
    B. Greenland   **D.** November

_____ **2.** The ship's captain used a
    A. radio   **C.** telephone
    B. light   **D.** surface

_____ **3.** The explosions sent up ash, dust, and hot
    A. food   **C.** ice
    B. rocks   **D.** fish

_____ **4.** The mountain grew into
    A. an island   **C.** a valley
    B. a nation   **D.** an iceberg

_____ **5.** The explosion came from
    A. an island   **C.** an earthquake
    B. a volcano   **D.** a fishing boat

The new island continued to grow for two years. It finally stopped in August of 1965. It was 550 feet high. It was more than a mile long and about six miles around.

The people of Iceland named the new island Surtsey. This name comes from an old myth. In the story Surtur was a mighty fire giant. People thought that Surtsey was also a giant by the time it stopped growing.

Scientists are very interested in Surtsey. It is the first new island to appear in the North Atlantic in two hundred years. Scientists want to learn more about how this happened. They are also studying how plant life begins on a new island. Another thing scientists want to know is how long Surtsey will last. They wonder whether the island will be destroyed by the same volcano that created it.

_____ **6.** The new island became quiet in
     A. 1956   **C.** the old story
     B. 1963   **D.** 1965

_____ **7.** Surtur was a fire giant in an old
     A. tale   **C.** snow
     B. island   **D.** volcano

_____ **8.** In the myth Surtur was
     A. cloudy   **C.** powerful
     B. weak   **D.** peaceful

_____ **9.** Scientists are studying
     A. plant life   **C.** people
     B. dead fish   **D.** animal life

_____**10.** Scientists also want to know how long Surtsey will
     A. return   **C.** burn
     B. remain   **D.** flood

Writing

Read the story below. Think about the facts. Then answer the questions in complete sentences.

> Sequoyah was a Cherokee. He was born in Tennessee around 1760. Other Cherokees looked up to his family for its knowledge of tribal traditions.
>
> At the time his tribe did not understand books that whites used. Some thought the paper "spoke" to whites. Sequoyah studied the books of white people. He then decided to create a writing system for his tribe. He worked on it for 12 years. At last it was done. His system was used to record tribal culture. It was also used to print newspapers. Thanks to Sequoyah, the Cherokee traditions were kept safe for future generations.

1. To what tribe did Sequoyah belong?

_____

_____

2. Why did people look up to Sequoyah's family?

_____

_____

3. How long did Sequoyah work on his writing system?

_____

_____

To check your answers, turn to page 60.

Prewriting

Think of an idea you might write about, such as a famous person or a famous event in history. Write the idea in the center of the idea web below. Then fill out the rest of the web with facts.

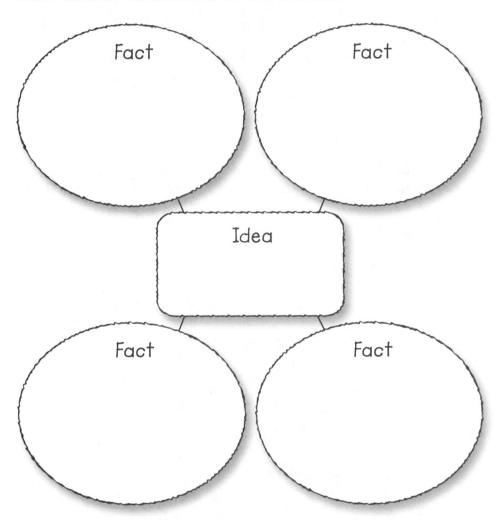

On Your Own

Now use another sheet of paper to write a paragraph about your idea. Use the facts from your idea web.

To check your answers, turn to page 60.

How to Box the Gnat

All over the country, many Americans are learning to "Dip for the Oyster," "Box the Gnat," and "Wring the Dishrag." These are special names for different movements in square dances.

A square-dance party may be called by many names. Such a party may be called a hog wrassle, a hoedown, a barndance, or a shindig. But all square dances are alike in certain ways. Four couples line up and face each other. A caller chants or sings directions. The dancers shuffle, glide, or run while people clap.

Pioneers in New England started these dances. As people moved westward and southward, new movements were added. In the Midwest, dancers created the "Grand Right and Left." In the far West, cowboys lifted their partners off the ground during "The Swing."

_____ **1.** The dance movements have special
  A. squares   **C.** shindigs
  B. names   **D.** boxes

_____ **2.** A hoedown is a kind of
  A. party   **C.** step
  B. sport   **D.** tool

_____ **3.** The caller gives
  A. parties   **C.** squares
  B. directions   **D.** barndances

_____ **4.** Square dancing started in
  A. the Far West   **C.** New England
  B. the South   **D.** the Midwest

_____ **5.** In "The Swing," men lifted their partners
  A. to the right   **C.** off the ground
  B. to the left   **D.** Grand Right and Left

Square dancing comes from dances done long ago in England. People there did *country dances*. In one country dance, dancers formed a circle. This dance was called a round. Another country dance was the longways. In this one, two long lines of dancers faced one another. A popular longways is called the Virginia Reel.

Around the year 1900, square dancing was dying out. Dancers liked the new *couple dancing* better. But in the 1940s, people became interested in the songs and dances the pioneers enjoyed. Square dancing became popular again. The interest in square dancing is still growing. But it's not easy to learn some of those movements! Square-dance contests award ribbons or badges to the winners. So if you're invited to a hog wrassle, get ready for music, action, and fun.

_____ **6.** In a round
- **A.** a circle is formed
- **B.** a longways is danced
- **C.** people wrestled
- **D.** people dance in Virginia

_____ **7.** The Virginia Reel is a
- **A.** longways
- **B.** square
- **C.** couple dance
- **D.** new name

_____ **8.** Between 1900 and 1940, couple dancing became
- **A.** impossible
- **B.** popular
- **C.** a round
- **D.** a longways

_____ **9.** Square dancing started again when people became
- **A.** interested in history
- **B.** better Americans
- **C.** tired of couples
- **D.** buyers of clothing

_____**10.** In a square-dance contest, people earn
- **A.** boots
- **B.** music
- **C.** difficult movements
- **D.** ribbons or badges

Camera Pioneers

Ilse Bing was a photographer in the 1930s. She was one of the first photographers to use a camera to make works of art. Cameras had been around since the late 1800s. However, most photographers used them to take pictures of news events or famous people. Bing took photos of people who were dressed beautifully or oddly.

At about the same time, Laura Gilpin was working in the American Southwest. She took pictures as she hiked through the desert. One of Gilpin's most famous pictures is called *Shiprock, New Mexico*. It shows a gigantic rock standing alone in a valley. Gilpin made many of her prints on a special soft paper. The special paper made her prints look cloudy and gray, like old paintings. That's the way Gilpin wanted her work to look.

_____ **1.** Ilse Bing was one of the first
    A. cameras   **C.** art photographers
    B. photographs   **D.** news events

_____ **2.** Bing wanted to take photographs that were
    A. art   **C.** news
    B. famous   **D.** first

_____ **3.** *Shiprock, New Mexico* is a
    A. picture   **C.** valley
    B. desert   **D.** ship

_____ **4.** Laura Gilpin worked in
    A. the Southwest   **C.** the South
    B. Germany   **D.** the West

_____ **5.** Gilpin wanted her pictures to look like
    A. soft paper   **C.** old paintings
    B. other photos   **D.** gray clouds

Bing chose subjects that were quite different from Gilpin's. She liked city life. She loved bright lights, big buildings, and constant movement. She took pictures in Germany and France. Then in 1941 she moved to New York City. Soon magazines were using her work.

Gilpin stayed in the Southwest. She made photo landscapes in black and white on special paper. She could make a river look like a black snake, curving through the white desert sand.

When Gilpin died, she left thousands of striking photographs. Bing's collection may be just as large. Museums now treasure their work. Photographs by Bing and Gilpin are shown in cities all over the world.

_____ 6. Bing took pictures of
     A. dresses   C. cities
     B. magazines   D. rivers

_____ 7. Gilpin made black-and-white photo landscapes with
     A. desert sand   C. city life
     B. special paper   D. curving snakes

_____ 8. In 1941 Bing moved to
     A. Germany   C. France
     B. the Southwest   D. New York City

_____ 9. Museums now think that Bing's and Gilpin's work is
     A. small   C. valuable
     B. dull   D. worthless

_____ 10. Photographs by Bing and Gilpin are shown
     A. only in Paris   C. only in the Southwest
     B. everywhere   D. in landscapes

A Great Poet

Elizabeth Barrett Browning was a famous poet. She was born in 1806 in England. As a child she was taught at home instead of at a school. She studied Greek and Latin at an early age. She also enjoyed writing poetry. Her father was very proud of her work. He had one of her long poems published when she was only 13.

At age 15 Elizabeth hurt her spine in a fall. Later when she was 32, her brother drowned in a swimming accident. That shock caused Elizabeth's health to grow much worse. She became a shy and quiet person. She spent most of her days alone in a darkened room. There she wrote long poems and letters. In 1844 a book of her poems was published. Another poet, Robert Browning, read the collection. He liked the poems so much that he wrote her a letter.

_____ **1.** Elizabeth Barrett Browning was born in
      A. 1806   **c.** 1832
      B. 1813   **D.** 1844

_____ **2.** At age 13 Elizabeth had a
      A. spine injury   **c.** new teacher
      B. book published   **D.** poem published

_____ **3.** After Elizabeth's accident, her brother
      A. drowned   **c.** married
      B. disappeared   **D.** was born

_____ **4.** Alone in her room, Elizabeth wrote
      A. nothing at all   **c.** short stories
      B. novels   **D.** long poems and letters

_____ **5.** Elizabeth received a letter from
      A. her father   **c.** Robert Browning
      B. her mother   **D.** the Queen of England

In 1845 Elizabeth and Robert became engaged, and they were married in Italy a year later. From then on, Elizabeth's health improved greatly. Her doctors were very surprised. She gave birth to a son three years later. The Brownings invited many famous artists and writers to their home in Italy.

Meanwhile Elizabeth kept on writing poems. Many were protests against things she felt were unfair in life. One poem attacked the use of child labor in England. But she also wrote love poems. Her most famous poem begins: "How do I love thee? Let me count the ways." Over time more books of her poems were published. Today many poetry lovers read and enjoy her works.

_____ **6.** After Elizabeth married, her health
- **A.** grew a little worse
- **B.** stayed the same
- **C.** grew much worse
- **D.** got much better

_____ **7.** The Brownings made their home in
- **A.** Italy
- **B.** England
- **C.** America
- **D.** France

_____ **8.** Elizabeth wrote many
- **A.** protest songs
- **B.** protest poems
- **C.** plays
- **D.** novels

_____ **9.** Elizabeth's best-known work is a
- **A.** protest poem
- **B.** love poem
- **C.** short story
- **D.** painting

_____ **10.** Elizabeth's works were published in
- **A.** newspapers
- **B.** magazines
- **C.** books
- **D.** posters

Home Sweet Home

How would you like to come home after a long day, open the door, and walk into an elephant? That's what you would do if you lived in Elephant House in Margate, New Jersey. The elephant-shaped house was built in 1881 by James Lafferty. In 1962 Herbert Green built a chicken-shaped house.

Sarah Winchester tried to build a ghost-proof house in San Jose, California. Workers built fake chimneys, doors that open onto blank walls, and stairs that lead nowhere. Many rooms were torn down and then rebuilt in a new way to confuse the ghosts. It took 38 years to complete the house!

Some houses are built of strange materials. A house in Pigeon Cove, Massachusetts, is built from more than one hundred thousand newspapers. In Canada, George Plumb built a house entirely out of bottles.

_____ **1.** The elephant-shaped house was built in
     A. 1881   **C.** 1922
     B. 1884   **D.** 1962

_____ **2.** Herbert Green's house is shaped like
     A. a chicken   **C.** an elephant
     B. a door   **D.** a pigeon

_____ **3.** Sarah Winchester built a house in
     A. Massachusetts   **C.** New Jersey
     B. California   **D.** Oklahoma

_____ **4.** Winchester tried to build a house that was
     A. a castle   **C.** rebuilt
     B. fool-proof   **D.** ghost-proof

_____ **5.** George Plumb's house is built of
     A. newspapers   **C.** chimneys
     B. aluminum cans   **D.** bottles

Some homes stand for great wealth and power. The Palace of Alhambra in Spain is one of the most beautiful homes in the world. The man who built it loved water. A stream runs through all nine acres of the palace. In each room there is a small pool of sparkling water.

Wealthy Americans design dream houses, too. In 1895 Cornelius Vanderbilt moved into a house named the Breakers. He called it his summer cottage. It cost ten million dollars to build and has walls trimmed with gold. This "summer cottage" could hold sixty guests comfortably.

Dream houses don't have to be expensive. A man named Baldasera built a house with ninety rooms for about three hundred dollars by digging under the earth. Baldasera worked alone. He spent about forty years completing his underground house.

_____ **6.** The Palace of Alhambra covers
  A. forty years **C.** ten million dollars
  B. nine acres **D.** ninety rooms

_____ **7.** The builder of the Palace of Alhambra loved
  A. water **C.** wealth and power
  B. chances to swim **D.** pools with lights

_____ **8.** Vanderbilt designed the Breakers to be his summer
  A. museum **C.** home
  B. camp **D.** dream

_____ **9.** Baldasera built his home
  A. in Spain **C.** without much money
  B. at the Breakers **D.** in a mountain

_____ **10.** To build his house, Baldasera needed much
  A. help **C.** time
  B. water **D.** money

Nature Paints a Turtle

A dozen small turtles slide off a rock and slip into the pond. These turtles look as if an artist had painted them. Pale yellow stripes cross their upper shells, and a red border circles the edge. More red and yellow stripes are on the turtles' heads, and just behind each eye is another yellow spot.

These eastern painted turtles live in slow-moving rivers, marshy areas, and ponds. They like to be in places where rocks and fallen trees project from the water. The turtles like to climb out onto the rocks or dead trees to sleep in the warm sunlight. If something frightens them, they slide quickly into the water.

Eastern painted turtles keep regular schedules. They nap at certain times, and they eat at certain times. In the late morning and the late afternoon, the turtles search for food.

_____ **1.** Eastern painted turtles are mainly red and
   A. green   **C.** blue
   B. orange   **D.** yellow

_____ **2.** These turtles live near rivers that are
   A. deep   **C.** slow
   B. warm   **D.** fast

_____ **3.** The turtles like to sleep
   A. in the sunlight **C.** inside trees
   B. under the water **D.** while eating

_____ **4.** The turtles move quickly when they are
   A. hungry   **C.** sleepy
   B. certain   **D.** frightened

_____ **5.** In the late afternoon, the turtles
   A. climb on rocks **C.** slide into the water
   B. search for food **D.** go swimming

Painted turtles eat almost anything they can find in their water homes. They feed on plants, insects, crayfish, and snails. Since young turtles need to grow fast, they usually eat more animal food than older turtles do. When winter comes, the turtles dig into the underwater mud and sleep there until warm weather returns.

Once a year, in the early summer, the females crawl to dry land. There they dig nests and lay their eggs. In about ten weeks, the young turtles hatch, and the real battle for life begins. As the turtles creep toward the water, many of them are caught and eaten by hungry raccoons, snakes, and bullfrogs.

Some varieties of young eastern painted turtles stay in their nests all through their first summer, fall, and winter. When they come out the following spring, they are larger, stronger, and quicker. Then they have a better chance of escaping their enemies.

_____

_____ **6.** To turtles, crayfish and snails are
     A. insects   **C.** enemies
     B. food   **D.** friends

_____ **7.** Animal food helps turtles
     A. grow quickly   **C.** eat more
     B. swim faster   **D.** sleep longer

_____ **8.** In the winter the turtles live
     A. close to water   **C.** under the mud
     B. on dry land   **D.** in warm homes

_____ **9.** Little turtles can be caught as they
     A. dig their nests   **C.** crawl toward water
     B. lay their eggs   **D.** hunt snakes

_____ **10.** Some varieties of turtles remain in their nests
     A. until they lay eggs   **C.** for about ten weeks
     B. for almost a year   **D.** to hide from raccoons

An Ugly Duckling

"What an ugly boy!" many people whispered when they saw Hans Christian Andersen. His hands and feet were gigantic. His eyes were tiny, and his nose was too big for such a thin face. He seemed clumsy as he clattered to school in his wooden shoes. Young Hans lived a sad life. His father was a poor shoemaker, and his mother was often ill. So the lonely boy created a make-believe world of his own, designing toy theaters and carving tiny figures to act in them.

In 1819, when Hans was 14, he made a big decision. He left his home and traveled across Denmark to the city of Copenhagen. "Here," declared Hans, "I will make my dream come true. I will become a famous actor." But it soon became evident that the dream would not come true at all. For three years Hans tried to find an acting job but had no luck. When he was 17, Hans sadly returned home.

_____ **1.** Hans Andersen's hands were
      A. small   **C.** gigantic
      B. thin   **D.** clumsy

_____ **2.** Andersen's father was
      A. lonely   **C.** ill
      B. poor   **D.** unkind

_____ **3.** Hans designed toy
      A. theaters   **C.** shoes
      B. books   **D.** plays

_____ **4.** In Copenhagen Hans could not find
      A. a perfect theater   **C.** a comfortable home
      B. an acting teacher   **D.** an acting job

_____ **5.** As he went home, Hans felt
      A. hopeful   **C.** famous
      B. sad   **D.** tired

Hans went back to school and worked hard at his lessons. He kept a journal, which he filled with his dreams, thoughts, and ideas for stories. In his journal Hans told about an ugly bird that was laughed at by the ducklings in a farmyard. But the little bird was not a duck at all, and it grew into an elegant swan.

Hans graduated from school with a new dream of becoming a famous writer of novels and articles. He kept busy at his writing. But publishers would not buy his books or news stories, and it seemed that this dream, too, would never come true. By the time he was thirty, Hans was very poor indeed. He decided to try writing stories for children. Adults and children loved these stories! People of all ages still do.

Perhaps the Andersen story that people know best is "The Ugly Duckling." In a way it is the story of Andersen himself.

_____ **6.** During his school days, Hans
    A. studied birds   **C.** became famous
    B. wrote lessons   **D.** recorded his thoughts

_____ **7.** The ugly bird was really a
    A. swan   **C.** student
    B. duckling   **D.** child

_____ **8.** Andersen could not sell his
    A. dreams   **C.** novels
    B. publishers   **D.** ducks

_____ **9.** Andersen started to write children's stories when he was
    A. in school   **C.** famous
    B. thirty   **D.** on a farm

_____ **10.** "The Ugly Duckling" may really be about Andersen's own
    A. school   **C.** fame
    B. life   **D.** ways

The Texas Camels

In May of 1856, a strange cargo walked off a naval ship at Old Powder Horn, Texas. The cargo was 33 camels from Arabia. A man named Hadji Ali led the camels onto the dock. He was an Arab "camel conductor." At that time few Americans had ever seen a camel. The animals were unfriendly. They spit, kicked, and snorted. Hadji Ali's job was to teach United States soldiers how to manage them.

Secretary of War Jefferson Davis brought the camels west to move supplies across the deserts. Mules, horses, and oxen were not always strong enough to make the trip. Camels were used for long desert voyages. They could go without water for many days. To find out how tough the camels really were, soldiers took 25 mules and 25 camels on a long, hard trip. The mules finally stumbled and fell. But the camels returned in good shape.

_____ **1.** The camels came to Texas on a
    A. truck   **C.** car
    B. train   **D.** ship

_____ **2.** Hadji Ali taught soldiers how to
    A. be conductors   **C.** make trips
    B. handle camels   **D.** fight wars

_____ **3.** Jefferson Davis wanted the camels to
    A. carry supplies   **C.** go without water
    B. climb ledges   **D.** work with mules

_____ **4.** Jefferson Davis was
    A. a ship captain   **C.** Secretary of the Army
    B. a soldier   **D.** Secretary of War

_____ **5.** The camels returned from the hard trip
    A. in fine shape   **C.** as tough as Davis
    B. on their knees   **D.** stumbling and falling

At first the camels were roped together in long lines. But when the lead camel tripped, all the other camels behind it tripped, too. Precious water was lost. The soldiers finally learned what Hadji Ali had told them. Camels will follow one another without being tied.

By 1861 the Civil War was sweeping the country. Confederate troops captured many Union Army camps in the West. They captured the camels, too. The soldiers did not know what to do with eighty camels. They used some to carry cotton to Mexico. But most of the camels were set free. They were just too hard to control. So the camels wandered alone in the desert. Once in a while, a surprised traveler would report seeing one. These reports died out after a few years, just as the camels did. As for Hadji Ali, he lived a long life in Arizona, where people called him Hi-Jolly.

_____ **6.** Water was spilled when
- **A.** soldiers cut ropes
- **C.** water was found
- **B.** a camel stumbled
- **D.** Hadji Ali left

_____ **7.** Camels will walk in a line without
- **A.** ropes
- **C.** leaders
- **B.** cliffs
- **D.** water

_____ **8.** The Confederate Army used camels to
- **A.** capture camps
- **C.** build circuses
- **B.** trick traders
- **D.** carry cotton

_____ **9.** After a few years, the camels
- **A.** chased travelers
- **C.** went home
- **B.** went to Mexico
- **D.** died out

_____ **10.** People in Arizona gave Hadji Ali
- **A.** a long life
- **C.** a new name
- **B.** another camel
- **D.** a good home

The Empty Hand

Many hundreds of years ago, a monk from India traveled to China. He began teaching people special movements to train the mind and body. His students learned to sit very still for a long time, breathing slowly. They learned shadow boxing and hand movements. All these movements came to be called kung-fu.

When a Japanese army invaded a Chinese island, kung-fu experts came to the rescue. They turned back the spears of the Japanese with their bare hands. The amazed Japanese called this weapon *kara* (empty) *te* (hand). Some Japanese then learned karate themselves, keeping it a secret for centuries. But after World War II, American soldiers discovered karate. The secret was no longer a secret. Teachers opened schools for people wanting to learn this ancient art. Today karate schools are all over the world.

_____ **1.** A monk came from India to
   A. China   **C.** America
   B. Japan   **D.** an island

_____ **2.** Kung-fu is a group of
   A. boxers   **C.** movements
   B. bodies   **D.** students

_____ **3.** Kung-fu experts turned back the
   A. secrets   **C.** movements
   B. spears   **D.** islands

_____ **4.** *Karate* is a
   A. Chinese word   **C.** Indian word
   B. American word   **D.** Japanese word

_____ **5.** Now karate schools are
   A. for fighters   **C.** for strong hands
   B. in Japan   **D.** all over the world

◯

Karate is excellent exercise. It is also a fine means of self-defense. Pupils learn more than fifty ways to throw off attackers. They learn to strike the forty vital points of the body to defend themselves.

Students spend three months just learning how to stretch, squat, sit, jump, and turn. They learn to kick forward and backward as high as an attacker's chin. Students also learn the art of complete stillness. For ten minutes of each hour, they kneel quietly. They think peaceful thoughts. This part is often the hardest to learn.

The black belt is the highest award a karate student can earn. There are nine other levels of black belt beyond the first one. Very few karate champions have ever gone beyond the first.

_____ **6.** Karate students learn how to
    A. find attackers   **C.** score forty points
    B. defend themselves   **D.** improve their nerves

_____ **7.** During the first three months, students learn how to
    A. stun people   **C.** kick backward
    B. win belts   **D.** lie down

_____ **8.** One of the hardest lessons is learning how to
    A. jump and turn   **C.** stretch and sit
    B. drop the class   **D.** kneel quietly

_____ **9.** The black belt is
    A. the highest award   **C.** sometimes too big
    B. the lowest award   **D.** easy to earn

_____ **10.** Few karate champions
    A. sit quietly   **C.** jump backward
    B. win ten levels   **D.** concentrate well

Hunter in the Sky

Stargazing takes imagination. People who love stargazing see the stars as shining spots in a dot-to-dot drawing game. They imagine lines that connect groups of stars called constellations. A constellation is a group of stars that looks like a person, an animal, or an object.

The constellation Orion is known as the hunter, after a hero from ancient Greek myths. To find Orion, first find the Big Dipper. The Big Dipper looks like a huge cup with a long handle. After you find the Big Dipper, turn around. There's Orion! He is outlined by four bright stars that form two triangles. The tips of the triangles seem to come together. Where they meet, there are three more bright stars. These form Orion's belt. Some fainter stars appear to hang from the belt. These are Orion's sword.

_____ **1.** When looking at a constellation, people try to imagine
- **A.** lines
- **B.** games
- **C.** spots
- **D.** groups

_____ **2.** Groups of stars are called
- **A.** stargazers
- **B.** ancient myths
- **C.** constellations
- **D.** connections

_____ **3.** Orion is named after a Greek
- **A.** object
- **B.** story
- **C.** animal
- **D.** hero

_____ **4.** The four bright stars in Orion form
- **A.** a big cup
- **B.** two triangles
- **C.** a long handle
- **D.** an animal

_____ **5.** Three bright stars form Orion's
- **A.** shoulder
- **B.** sword
- **C.** belt
- **D.** spear

Steck-Vaughn • Comprehension Skills Series

Different kinds of stars are in the constellation Orion. The star Betelgeuse makes Orion's right shoulder. *Betelgeuse* is an Arabic word that means "shoulder of the giant." The star itself is so huge that it is called a supergiant. Its diameter is four hundred times greater than that of our sun. Betelgeuse is considered a cool star. It is probably not as hot as our sun.

Rigel is the star that makes Orion's left foot. *Rigel* is the Arabic word for *foot*. Rigel is much brighter than Betelgeuse because it is much hotter. It's more than three times as hot as our sun. However, Rigel is just a baby in size compared to Betelgeuse.

A large, misty area near Orion's sword is called a nebula. It is a mass of shining gas and dust. The gases whirl together and may form new stars. As the new stars begin to shine, Orion will be brighter than ever.

_____ **6.** Betelgeuse makes
    A. Arabic words   **C.** different stars
    B. Orion's shoulder   **D.** huge sizes

_____ **7.** Betelgeuse is much larger than
    A. our sun   **C.** a diameter
    B. a supergiant   **D.** any nebula

_____ **8.** Rigel is brighter because it is
    A. bigger   **C.** hotter
    B. smaller   **D.** cooler

_____ **9.** Near Orion's sword is
    A. a cool star   **C.** a new star
    B. strange material   **D.** a nebula

_____ **10.** Orion may shine brighter
    A. when Rigel explodes   **C.** as dust shines
    B. as new stars shine   **D.** as dust forms

The Great Fire

It was 5:00 in the morning on April 18, 1906. The city of San Francisco was sleeping. At 5:13 an earthquake shattered the peace. The ground shifted, and streets buckled. Water and sewer pipes broke apart. Buildings crumbled.

Two smaller earthquakes quickly followed. The city's electrical wires fell. The broken, sputtering wires set off a fire that devoured the city. Screaming people ran to the parks and the bay to escape the fire.

San Francisco's six hundred firefighters went into action. But they could not fill their hoses from the broken water pipes. The only water was in San Francisco Bay. Soon even this water was not enough. The fire reached the city's gas house. It exploded, becoming a gigantic fireball. Flames joined flames. The firefighters almost lost all hope.

_____

_____ **1.** The earthquake hit San Francisco in the early
      A. afternoon   **C.** morning
      B. evening   **D.** night

_____ **2.** The fire was set off by
      A. broken sewer pipes   **C.** crumbled buildings
      B. fallen wires   **D.** the gas house

_____ **3.** People ran to the parks to find
      A. safety   **C.** buildings
      B. hoses   **D.** action

_____ **4.** The firefighters could only use water from
      A. water pipes   **C.** fire engines
      B. the bay   **D.** the gas house

_____ **5.** The firefighters almost lost hope when the
      A. pipes broke   **C.** wires fell
      B. gas house exploded   **D.** people screamed

The firefighters tried to stop the fire by making a firebreak, a cleared strip of land. They used dynamite to knock down a long row of buildings, hoping the fire would die out when it reached the cleared land. But this firebreak did not work.

For two days the fire raged. On April 20 the firefighters used cannons to make a much larger firebreak. They flattened beautiful homes along Van Ness Avenue. The cannon shells dug a ditch five hundred feet wide and almost a mile long. But high winds helped the flames leap over the huge ditch. More cannons were fired, and more mansions fell. Finally the fire was stopped. In three days, more than twenty-five thousand buildings and five square miles of the city had been destroyed. Over seven hundred people lost their lives.

On April 21 a soft rain fell. The hot ashes cooled, and the citizens of San Francisco began to rebuild.

_____ **6.** A firebreak is made by
    A. stopping the fire   **C.** using water hoses
    B. clearing the land   **D.** calling firefighters

_____ **7.** The firefighters made the first firebreak by using
    A. buildings   **C.** strips
    B. dynamite   **D.** ditches

_____ **8.** Buildings on Van Ness Avenue were destroyed by
    A. raging fire   **C.** cannon shells
    B. high winds   **D.** hot ashes

_____ **9.** When the fire came to the second firebreak, it
    A. exploded   **C.** did not burn
    B. died out   **D.** jumped a ditch

_____ **10.** The fire lasted
    A. weeks   **C.** hours
    B. months   **D.** days

Music of the Mind

When Ludwig van Beethoven was 28 years old, he wrote a letter to a friend. "Do not tell anyone I am losing my hearing," wrote Beethoven. "Each day it grows worse. I notice the hearing loss most when I am with people. I cannot hear what they are saying, so I cannot answer them. I fear that people think I am unfriendly."

This letter was written in 1801. By that time Beethoven already had composed music for the piano and for small groups of instruments. He also had finished his first symphony. A symphony is a long piece of music for a full orchestra.

In spite of his growing deafness, Beethoven continued to write lovely music. For many years, he even conducted orchestras. However, by the year 1822, his hearing was gone. But this did not stop him from composing. Much of his best music was written after he could no longer hear at all.

_____ 1. Beethoven's letter told about losing his
     A. music   **C.** secret
     B. hearing   **D.** friendships

_____ 2. By 1801 Beethoven had already
     A. written much music   **C.** given up conducting
     B. become totally deaf   **D.** sent more letters

_____ 3. Symphonies are played by
     A. pianos   **C.** small groups
     B. full orchestras   **D.** one instrument

_____ 4. After 1822 Beethoven could no longer
     A. compose   **C.** write
     B. sing   **D.** hear

_____ 5. Beethoven wrote much of his best music after he
     A. wrote symphonies   **C.** conducted people
     B. wrote letters   **D.** could not hear

How could a deaf musician continue to create such fine work? The answer probably is that Beethoven could always hear the music in his head. Then he wrote down what he heard.

Beethoven kept to a strict schedule. He got up at dawn and wrote music until late afternoon. Now and then he walked in his garden and thought about his compositions. He never let anyone see his symphonies until they were completed.

Beethoven tried out his written piano pieces as he worked on them. He had his piano changed so that it played very loudly. He also used a special stick. He held one end of the stick in his mouth and rested the other end on the piano strings. As he touched the piano keys with his fingers, he could feel the strong vibrations made by the strings. The vibrations were carried along the stick. This way, Beethoven *felt* the beautiful music that he could hear only in his mind.

_____ **6.** Beethoven wrote music that he heard
    A. in a garden   **C.** in his mind
    B. with other people   **D.** in the morning

_____ **7.** Beethoven took walks and
    A. picked flowers   **C.** thought about music
    B. kept a diary   **D.** hid his symphonies

_____ **8.** The musician touched the keys of the piano with
    A. his hands   **C.** a stick
    B. his mouth   **D.** a string

_____ **9.** The stick allowed Beethoven to
    A. play loudly   **C.** fix pianos
    B. feel music   **D.** write better

_____ **10.** Beethoven used the stick
    A. when walking   **C.** to scare dogs
    B. to feel vibrations   **D.** to keep time

A Great All-Around Athlete

Jim Thorpe was a Native American born in Oklahoma in 1888. His great-grandfather was Black Hawk, a famous chief. In school Jim proved to be a great athlete. He led his school team to fame in football. He won honors as a runner, kicker, and tackler.

In 1912 Thorpe took part in the Olympics. He became the first athlete ever to win two major track and field events at the games. Sadly, his gold medals were taken back a month later. Olympic officials believed that Thorpe had been paid when he played baseball before the games. They said that made him a pro player, so he never should have taken part in the games. Many fans were upset by the ruling. Years later the ruling was changed. Thorpe was again counted as a 1912 winner.

_____ **1.** Jim Thorpe was born in
   A. 1808   **C.** 1912
   B. 1880   **D.** 1888

_____ **2.** Thorpe's great-grandfather was a famous
   A. chief   **C.** football player
   B. baseball player   **D.** Olympic athlete

_____ **3.** Thorpe won honors as a runner and
   A. kicker and passer   **C.** kicker and tackler
   B. tackler and passer **D.** catcher and tackler

_____ **4.** At the Olympics Thorpe won two major events in
   A. baseball   **C.** track and field
   B. football   **D.** basketball

_____ **5.** Thorpe's gold medals were taken back
   A. a week later   **C.** a year later
   B. a month later **D.** years later

From 1913 to 1919, Thorpe played baseball on three major league teams. In 1915 he began a career as a pro football player, too. He played on seven teams over the next 15 years. Thorpe was a well-loved player. He helped to make football the popular game that it is today.

Thorpe cared a great deal about the game of football. He wished for players to be treated fairly by team owners. In 1920 he became the first president of a new football league for pro teams. Today it is known as the National Football League.

Jim Thorpe is still remembered as an outstanding athlete. Some people regard him as the best all-around athlete who ever lived.

_____ **6.** From 1913 to 1919, Thorpe played
  A. pro football   **C.** pro baseball
  B. pro basketball   **D.** pro hockey

_____ **7.** For 15 years Thorpe played on
  A. five football teams   **C.** two football teams
  B. seven football teams   **D.** three baseball teams

_____ **8.** Thorpe wanted pro football players to
  A. receive raises   **C.** be treated fairly
  B. be on television   **D.** go to college first

_____ **9.** Thorpe became a new football league's
  A. player   **C.** coach
  B. team owner   **D.** president

_____ **10.** Many consider Thorpe to be the greatest
  A. overall athlete   **C.** college student
  B. president   **D.** official

From Spanish to English

Are you able to speak Spanish? Even if you answer no, you may know more Spanish than you think. That's because many words in English come from the Spanish language.

Take the word *potato*, for example. The potato first came from South America, where it was called *patata*. In the 1500s the vegetable was brought to England. It was given the name *potato*.

Likewise, the name *tomato* comes from Spanish. This fruit was first eaten by the Nahuatl natives in Mexico. They called the food *tomatl*. In the 1500s Spanish priests brought the food to Europe. It was given the name *tomato*.

_____ **1.** The potato first came from
      A. North America   **C.** South Africa
      B. South America   **D.** South Carolina

_____ **2.** In the 1500s the potato was brought to
      A. Europe   **C.** England
      B. Mexico   **D.** the United States

_____ **3.** The name *tomato* comes from
      A. English   **C.** French
      B. Italian   **D.** Spanish

_____ **4.** Tomatoes were first eaten by
      A. American settlers   **C.** Spanish explorers
      B. Nahuatl natives   **D.** English colonists

_____ **5.** Spanish priests brought tomatoes to Europe in
      A. the 1600s   **C.** the 1500s
      B. the 1200s   **D.** the 1400s

Besides food terms, many cowboy words come from Spanish. That's because Western cowboys copied the ways of Mexican cowboys. For example, a rope in Spanish is *la reata*. The English word for the same rope became *lariat*. The type of pants that Mexican cowboys wore were called *chaparajos*. In English the term was shortened to *chaps*.

Many places in the United States have Spanish names as well. Spanish pioneers settled the town of Los Angeles, whose name means "the angels." The Spanish also settled the town of Santa Fe, whose name means "holy faith." The state of Florida got its name from the Spanish word *flor*, meaning "flower."

_____ **6.** Spanish is the source of many American
      A. baseball terms   **C.** music terms
      B. sailing terms   **D.** cowboy terms

_____ **7.** The words *la reata* and *lariat* both mean
      A. pants   **C.** cowboy
      B. rope   **D.** chaps

_____ **8.** A city whose name means "the angels" is
      A. Los Angeles   **C.** St. Louis
      B. Santa Fe   **D.** Florida City

_____ **9.** Santa Fe was settled by
      A. United States citizens   **C.** Spanish pioneers
      B. English colonists   **D.** the King of England

_____ **10.** The *Flor* in Florida means
      A. "river"   **C.** "saint"
      B. "faith"   **D.** "flower"

Writing

Read the story below. Think about the facts. Then answer the questions in complete sentences.

> Have you ever seen the Statue of Liberty? It is a tall figure of a robed woman holding a torch. She stands proudly on Liberty Island in New York Harbor. The statue is a symbol of freedom for the United States. It was given as a gift to the United States by France in 1884.
>
> The statue is one of the largest ever built. It stands 151 feet high from its base to the top of the torch. When the statue was shipped to America, it could not be sent in one piece. Instead it was taken apart and packed in 214 separate crates.

1. What is the Statue of Liberty?

_____

_____

2. Who gave the statue to the United States?

_____

_____

3. How tall is the statue?

_____

_____

To check your answers, turn to page 60.

Prewriting

Think of an idea you might write about, such as a building in your town or a place you once visited. Write the idea in the center of the idea web below. Then fill out the rest of the web with facts.

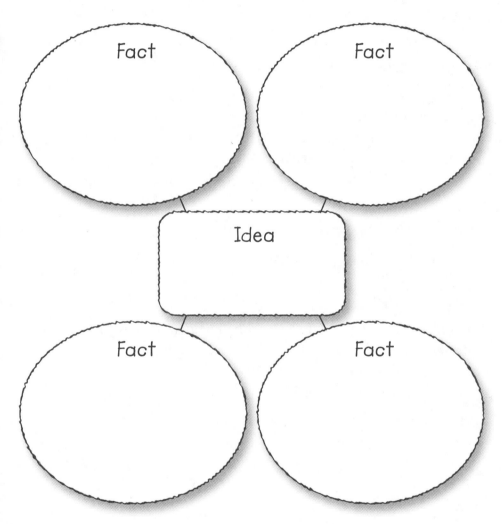

Fact

Fact

Idea

Fact

Fact

On Your Own

Now use another sheet of paper to write a paragraph about your idea. Use the facts from your idea web.

To check your answers, turn to page 60.

Check Yourself

What Are Facts? Page 2
Fact: December 1903
Fact: Orville Wright

Practice Finding Facts, Page 3
3. B

To check your answers to pages 6–29, see page 61.

Writing, Page 30
Possible answers include:
1. Sequoyah belonged to the Cherokee tribe.
2. His family was respected for its knowledge of tribal traditions.
3. Sequoyah worked on his writing system for 12 years.

Writing, Page 31
Check that you have four facts in your paragraph.

To check your answers to pages 32–57, see page 62.

Writing, Page 58
Possible answers include:
1. The Statue of Liberty is a figure of a robed woman holding a torch.
2. France gave the statue to the United States as a gift.
3. The statue is 151 feet tall.

Writing, Page 59
Check that you have four facts in your paragraph.

Steck-Vaughn • Comprehension Skills Series

Check Yourself

Unit 1 pp. 6–7	Unit 2 pp. 8–9	Unit 3 pp. 10–11	Unit 4 pp. 12–13	Unit 5 pp. 14–15	Unit 6 pp. 16–17	Unit 7 pp. 18–19	Unit 8 pp. 20–21	Unit 9 pp. 22–23	Unit 10 pp. 24–25	Unit 11 pp. 26–27	Unit 12 pp. 28–29
1. B	**1.** C	**1.** B	**1.** C	**1.** C	**1.** D	**1.** D	**1.** B	**1.** C	**1.** C	**1.** D	**1.** C
2. C	**2.** A	**2.** D	**2.** A	**2.** B	**2.** B	**2.** B	**2.** C	**2.** B	**2.** D	**2.** D	**2.** A
3. A	**3.** C	**3.** A	**3.** D	**3.** D	**3.** D	**3.** A	**3.** C	**3.** C	**3.** A	**3.** B	**3.** B
4. C	**4.** B	**4.** C	**4.** A	**4.** C	**4.** A	**4.** C	**4.** A	**4.** D	**4.** C	**4.** B	**4.** A
5. D	**5.** D	**5.** A	**5.** D	**5.** B	**5.** C	**5.** A	**5.** C	**5.** A	**5.** C	**5.** A	**5.** B
6. B	**6.** B	**6.** C	**6.** B	**6.** D	**6.** D	**6.** D	**6.** D	**6.** C	**6.** B	**6.** C	**6.** D
7. A	**7.** A	**7.** B	**7.** B	**7.** A	**7.** B	**7.** C	**7.** A	**7.** A	**7.** C	**7.** C	**7.** A
8. C	**8.** B	**8.** D	**8.** C	**8.** B	**8.** C	**8.** A	**8.** B	**8.** C	**8.** D	**8.** D	**8.** C
9. A	**9.** D	**9.** C	**9.** B	**9.** B	**9.** B	**9.** C	**9.** A	**9.** B	**9.** D	**9.** B	**9.** A
10. D	**10.** C	**10.** A	**10.** D	**10.** C	**10.** A	**10.** C	**10.** C	**10.** C	**10.** C	**10.** A	**10.** B

Unit 13 pp. 32–33	Unit 14 pp. 34–35	Unit 15 pp. 36–37	Unit 16 pp. 38–39	Unit 17 pp. 40–41	Unit 18 pp. 42–43	Unit 19 pp. 44–45	Unit 20 pp. 46–47	Unit 21 pp. 48–49	Unit 22 pp. 50–51	Unit 23 pp. 52–53	Unit 24 pp. 54–55	Unit 25 pp. 56–57
1. B	1. C	1. A	1. A	1. D	1. C	1. D	1. A	1. A	1. C	1. B	1. D	1. B
2. A	2. A	2. D	2. A	2. C	2. B	2. B	2. C	2. C	2. B	2. A	2. A	2. C
3. B	3. A	3. A	3. B	3. A	3. A	3. A	3. B	3. D	3. A	3. B	3. C	3. D
4. C	4. A	4. D	4. D	4. D	4. D	4. D	4. D	4. B	4. B	4. D	4. C	4. B
5. C	5. C	5. C	5. D	5. B	5. B	5. A	5. D	5. C	5. B	5. D	5. B	5. C
6. A	6. C	6. D	6. B	6. B	6. D	6. B	6. B	6. B	6. B	6. C	6. C	6. D
7. A	7. B	7. A	7. A	7. A	7. A	7. A	7. C	7. A	7. B	7. C	7. B	7. B
8. B	8. D	8. B	8. C	8. C	8. C	8. D	8. D	8. C	8. C	8. A	8. C	8. A
9. A	9. C	9. B	9. C	9. C	9. B	9. D	9. A	9. D	9. D	9. B	9. D	9. C
10. D	10. B	10. C	10. C	10. B	10. B	10. C	10. B	10. B	10. D	10. B	10. A	10. D